Who Should I Date?

Relationship Advice for the Real World

William P. Smith

New Growth Press
www.newgrowthpress.com

All Scripture quotations, unless otherwise indicated, are taken from the *Holy Bible,* New International Version®, NIV®. Copyright © 1973, 1978, 1984 by International Bible Society. Used by permission of Zondervan. All rights reserved.

New Growth Press, Greensboro, NC 27429
Copyright © 2009 by Christian Counseling & Educational Foundation
All rights reserved. Published 2009.

Typesetting: Robin Black, www.blackbirdcreative.biz

ISBN-10: 1-935273-00-0
ISBN-13: 978-1-935273-00-4

Library of Congress Cataloging-in-Publication Data

Smith, William P., 1965-
 Who should I date? : relationship advice for the real world / William P. Smith.
   p. cm.
 Includes bibliographical references and index.
 ISBN-13: 978-1-935273-00-4
 ISBN-10: 1-935273-00-0
 1. Single people—Religious life. 2. Single people—Conduct of life. 3. Dating (Social customs)—Religious aspects—Christianity. 4. Man-woman relationships--Religious aspects—Christianity. I. Title.
 BV4596.S5S65 2009
 248.8′4—dc22

                                         2009016563

Printed in Canada

16 15 14 13 12 11 10   2 3 4 5

FSC
Mixed Sources
Cert no. SW-COC-000952
© 1996 FSC

Your mother always said there were lots of fish in the sea—but how do you know which ones to keep and which ones to throw back? You have so many choices. What do you look for? A tingly feeling? Excitement? A sense of belonging?

Those feelings are wonderful, but do they mean that you have found someone to spend time with? Or even more, to settle down with? How do you know when to hang on to someone and when to let her go? What separates Mr. Right from Mr. Oh-So-Wrong?

It's easy to look for the wrong things when you are searching for a meaningful relationship. You might be drawn to someone who is fun, good-looking, and interested in the same things as you. Those things aren't necessarily bad, but on their own they can't give you the full picture. God's criteria for choosing friends looks below the surface and focuses on their character (Psalm 119:63; Proverbs 17:7). You can become consumed with focusing on which character traits are the most important, but since they are all variations of the same theme, simply look for someone who knows how to love well. The apostle Paul gives a great description of what real love is in 1 Corinthians 13:4–7:

> Love is patient, love is kind. It does not envy,
> it does not boast, it is not proud. It is not rude,
> it is not self-seeking, it is not easily angered,
> it keeps no record of wrongs. Love does not
> delight in evil but rejoices with the truth. It
> always protects, always trusts, always hopes,
> always perseveres.

The character traits listed below are all practical expressions of the kind of love that Paul is describing. So look for them, and use their presence (or absence!) to help you decide whether to pursue your friendship further. You might not notice them the first time you go bowling or see a play, but they won't take long to emerge. Read through this list, and keep these qualities in mind as you get to know other people.

Actively Listens vs. Passively Hears

Active listening is hard work; it requires effort and practice. It means putting aside your interests and tuning into someone else's reality and experience. Active listening is self-forgetting instead of self-seeking. It's a practical expression of one of the most important qualities of a Christian: looking out for the interests of others (Philippians 2:4).

Passive hearing is easy. You simply allow the other person to become background noise, and let him drone on like a 2:00 AM vacuum cleaner infomercial. You treat him as a necessary but unwanted intrusion, and wait impatiently for him to finish so you can return to your more interesting, self-oriented life. How do you experience your friend: As someone who does the hard work of listening? Or as someone who only hears you?

Constructively Disagrees or Is Just Disagreeable?

God made us to be life-long learners, and one of the primary ways we learn is from each other. Wise people love to be instructed and taught, so they aren't threatened when you disagree with them (Proverbs 9:8–9). Instead, they use a disagreement as a way to learn wisdom, and they wisely speak their mind.

Some people, however, are just disagreeable. They are always looking to pick a fight; they always have to be right; and they always have to get their own way. A disagreeable person builds her sense of superiority, security, and self-worth through arguing, never admitting she might be wrong. How does your friend handle disagreements? Is she learning through them or just trying to prove her point? Remember, love is "not easily angered."

Helps You Sound Your Best vs. Your Worst

Have you experienced someone helping you put your feelings into words? Or have you ever exclaimed, "That's what I was thinking, but I couldn't get it out!" Such wonderful experiences take place when someone is committed to helping you be your best.

Sadly, you've probably also experienced someone who frustrated your attempts to put your thoughts into words. Remember how you felt when he kept cutting you off before you finished what you were trying to say? Or how you felt when she made you sound ridiculous? That only happens when your friend is committed to being the best *he* can be, even if it's at your expense.

Is Giving vs. Needy

People have different motives for getting into a relationship. Some want to give of themselves so they and their friends will be stronger. God says in his Word that, in this kind of relationship, "Two are better than one.…If one falls down, his friend can help him up" (Ecclesiastes 4:9–10). Other people want to have friends because they hope their friends will complete them. They are needy—wanting to belong, to be cared for, to look successful—and they want others to meet their needs. The apostle Paul explains the difference in his letter to the Galatians: "You, my brothers, were called to be free. But do not use your freedom to indulge the sinful nature; rather, serve one another in love. The entire law is summed up in a single command: 'Love your neighbor as yourself.' If you keep on biting and devouring each other, watch out or you will be destroyed by each other" (Galatians 5:13–15).

A good way to find out if someone is a giving friend or a needy one is by considering the quantity and quality of his present relationships. Think about how she cares for her close friends and how long she has had those friendships. Consider how he relates to his family: Is he involved in their lives? Is she regularly involved in serving her friends, her church, and her community? Does he serve joyfully without expecting a return, or does it seem that he is giving in hopes of getting something back?

Is Patient vs. Intemperate

Many years ago I was in a store watching a mother struggle with her young daughter. As the child zipped away one more time to pursue what had caught her attention, her exasperated mother yelled, "Patience!" The little girl looked up—having heard her name. The absurd activity of yelling (*not* a patient activity) *at* Patience nearly had me laughing out loud, and I silently vowed to give careful thought before naming my children!

Everyone on this planet, just like Patience's mom, experiences frustration. The important thing is how we react when the world doesn't go our way. Intemperate people don't live as if God is actively involved in their world. When their life doesn't line up according to their desires, they express their irritation with explosions of anger, grimaces of disgust, and sighs of hopelessness.

What does your friend's standard operating mode tell you about his functional belief in God's sovereignty? What characterizes her? Would you say she's more likely to be cranky, irritable, and short-fused or patient, longsuffering, and even-tempered?

Willingly Confesses vs. Being Cornered

Every relationship in this fallen world has at least two sinners in it. So if we want lasting relationships, we have to deal with our failure to love each other well. Honest communication and grace-driven forgiveness are essential, but so is freely offered confession.

If you have to hound someone into a corner, tie him down, and beat a confession out of him, there is little hope your relationship will enjoy the open honesty so necessary to building mutual trust and confidence. People who know their sins have been forgiven by the Supreme Judge will willingly—even if not easily—confess their sins to each other.

Jesus: The Only Foundation That Lasts

Since all of these character traits are expressions of love, to grow in them you and your friend have to know Jesus. The Bible tells us that "God is love," and Jesus is the "exact imprint" of God (1 John 4:8; Hebrews 1:3 ESV). So the foundation of your relationship has to be your mutual life of faith in Christ. A relationship without Christ will be as unstable as a house on the sand. But if you build your relationship on the rock of Jesus Christ, you will have the foundation to withstand life's storms (Matthew 7:24–27).

Unfortunately, many people build their relationships with the opposite sex on a superficial foundation of romantic feelings. It is true that spending time with a special person is a blessing from God. It's a small taste of heaven, where you will love and enjoy God and people forever. But, you can't build a lasting relationship only on your feelings for each other. You need the much stronger material of a relationship built on your love for God and others.

So look for someone whose life is centered on Jesus. And make sure that your life is centered on Christ also. Remember: we tend to attract and be attracted to people of our own maturity. More mature people do spend time caring and ministering to those of lesser maturity, but they look elsewhere when developing an inner circle of friends. If you want to date a mature Christian, then you need to ask God to show you how to become a mature Christian who loves others well.

Practical Strategies for Change

Rather than casually falling into a relationship, start by asking yourself at the beginning of a friendship, *Should this relationship take the next step in becoming more serious?* To help you make that decision, take this short relationship readiness quiz. Fill in the blanks with your friend's name first, and then retake the quiz and put your own name in the blank. As you take the quiz keep the following things in mind:

- What do your answers tell you about your friend? We all need to grow in each of these areas, so look for trends in your friend's life, not perfection.
- What do your answers tell you about yourself? Do you have the qualities that you are looking for in someone else?

- What areas in your life do you sense Jesus calling you to work on in your present relationships? What will you do to bring that about?

Relationship Readiness Quiz

1. Is _____ an active listener?

    - Does he indicate with his body (leaning forward, making regular eye-contact, nodding his head) that he's engaged in what you're saying?
    - Does she ask questions that allow you to explore what you're saying, thinking, and feeling?
    - Does he check with you to find out if he's understood you?

2. Or, is _____ a passive hearer?

    - Does she look disinterested (arms folded, eyes focused elsewhere, fidgeting)?

- Does he interrupt you?
- Is she waiting for you to get done, so that she can tell you about what happened to her?

3. Does _____ disagree in healthy ways?

- Does she voice her differing opinions in a non-threatening manner?
- Do his disagreements with you help you see the world in a different way?
- Does she invite you to challenge her?

4. Or, is _____ simply disagreeable?

- Are disagreements an opportunity for him to win while you lose?
- Does she have the last word on most topics?
- Does he grow cold and silent when you disagree?

5. Does _____ make you sound your best?

- Does he help you clarify your thoughts?
- Does she suggest ways your thoughts could be firmer or your ideas better?
- Does he help you think through the pros as well as the cons of your position?

6. Or, does _____ make you sound your worst?

- Does she ridicule your position?
- Does he mimic your voice and gestures?
- Does she cut you off and object before you've finished laying out your thoughts?

7. Is _____ a giving person?

- Does she keep up with old friends and make new ones?
- Does he like to serve other people?
- Does she maintain regular, but not excessive, contact with her family?

8. Or, is _____ a needy person?

- Does he regularly reject your attempts to get together with more people than just you?
- Do you feel smothered by the attention she gives you?
- Are all of his active relationships less than three years old?

9. Is _____ patient in the face of frustrations?

- Is he slow to anger?
- Does she attempt to give others the benefit of the doubt?
- Does he investigate matters before drawing conclusions?

10. Or, is _____ intemperate?

- Does she quickly take offense—even at little things?

- Does he explode? Does she grow bitter and silent?
- Does he assume the worst about others when things don't go his way?

11. Does _____ graciously confess his failings?

- Does she regularly acknowledge areas of her life that need change?
- Does he spontaneously confess when he wrongs you?
- Does she tell you how the Holy Spirit is convicting her?

12. Does _____ have to be cornered?

- Do you have to catch him before he admits wrongs?
- Does she regularly defend herself, arguing that what she did was right?

- Does he make all of his sins sound as though they took place in the (distant) past?

How did your friend do on the quiz? Just as importantly, how did you do? Of course you noticed that you and your friend have deficiencies in all these areas. Compared to Jesus we're all immature in our personalities, and we all need to grow in becoming more like him. We will make mistakes and sin against each other. That's a given. You won't find the perfect person, but that's okay because you aren't perfect either. Instead of looking for the perfect person, look for someone who is open to God's Spirit confronting him, guiding him, and teaching him.

Don't Be in a Rush

Remember that you don't have to rush into a serious relationship with the first person you are attracted to. Instead, give yourself plenty of time to get to know lots of people in many different settings.

Don't let your desire for a romantic relationship cloud your judgment. Many people have been hurt by forming a deep emotional connection with someone they really didn't know very well. It is worse to be involved with someone immature than not to have someone at all. Sometimes the feeling of not being wanted is so overpowering that you are tempted to go out with anyone. But I have talked to many people who feel trapped in bad relationships because they were desperate for *any* relationship.

So if you meet someone you are interested in, consider getting to know him or her better by doing a combination of things in groups—fun activities, service projects, Bible studies—instead of only pairing off for more traditional dating activities. The more natural contexts will allow you to see more dimensions of someone's personality and character. That knowledge will help you be more intentional in developing good romantic attachments. Another safeguard for you would be to find an older, wiser Christian who can help you think through how you are approaching your relationships and give you guidance as you develop them.

God made us to be in relationship with others, but your most important relationship is with him. In human relationships you get a taste of the happiness, meaning, and fulfillment that ultimately are only to be found, in their fullest form, in him. So don't let yourself be fooled into believing that a romantic relationship will be the most satisfying experience of your life. Instead, thank God for the tastes that you have had that remind you of what his love is like, and ask him to give you a desire for a deeper and more intimate relationship with him. Trust him with your hopes for a relationship and ask for his wisdom and guidance when you enter into one. Most of all, ask him to fill you with his Spirit so you can continue growing in your ability to love others.

If you were helped by reading this booklet, perhaps you or someone you know would also be encouraged by these booklets:

Angry Children: Understanding and Helping Your Child Regain Control, Michael R. Emlet, M.Div., M.D.

Conflict: A Redemptive Opportunity, Timothy S. Lane, M.Div., D.Min.

Divorce Recovery: Growing and Healing God's Way, Winston T. Smith, M.Div.

Eating Disorders: The Quest for Thinness, Edward T. Welch, M.Div., Ph.D.

Facing Death with Hope: Living for What Lasts, David Powlison, M.Div., Ph.D.

Family Feuds: How to Respond, Timothy S. Lane, M.Div., D.Min.

Freedom from Guilt: Finding Release from Your Burdens, Timothy S. Lane, M.Div., D.Min.

Forgiving Others: Joining Wisdom and Love, Timothy S. Lane, M.Div., D.Min.

Healing after Abortion: God's Mercy Is for You, David Powlison, M.Div., Ph.D.

Help for Stepfamilies: Avoiding the Pitfalls and Learning to Love, Winston T. Smith, M.Div.

Help for the Caregiver: Facing the Challenges with Understanding and Strength, Michael R. Emlet, M.Div., M.D.

Helping Your Adopted Child: Understanding Your Child's Unique Identity, Paul David Tripp, M.Div., D.Min.

Help! My Spouse Committed Adultery: First Steps for Dealing with Betrayal, Winston T. Smith, M.Div.

How Do I Stop Losing It with My Kids? Getting to the Heart of Your Discipline Problems, William P. Smith, M.Div., Ph.D.

How to Love Difficult People: Receiving and Sharing God's Mercy, William P. Smith, M.Div., Ph.D.

It's All about Me: The Problem with Masturbation, Winston T. Smith, M.Div.

Living with an Angry Spouse: Help for Victims of Abuse, Edward T. Welch, M.Div., Ph.D.

Peer Pressure: Recognizing the Warning Signs and Giving New Direction, Paul David Tripp, M.Div., D.Min.

Recovering from Child Abuse: Healing and Hope for Victims, David Powlison, M.Div., Ph.D.

Renewing Marital Intimacy: Closing the Gap Between You and Your Spouse, David Powlison, M.Div., Ph.D.

Restoring Your Broken Marriage: Healing after Adultery, Robert D. Jones, M.Div., D.Min.

Should We Get Married? How to Evaluate Your Relationship, William P. Smith, M.Div., Ph.D.

Single Parents: Daily Grace for the Hardest Job, Robert D. Jones, M.Div., D.Min.

When Bad Things Happen: Thoughtful Answers to Hard Questions, William P. Smith, M.Div., Ph.D.

When the Money Runs Out: Hope and Help for the Financially Stressed, James C. Petty, M.Div., D.Min.

Who Does the Dishes? Decision Making in Marriage, Winston T. Smith, M.Div.

To learn more about CCEF, visit our website at www.ccef.org